C0 1 69 68906 X5

C000255125

How to make your own soap

Joy James

This book is dedicated to my Guardian Angel, without whom
it would never have been written. I'd also like to thank all my
friends and family for their support and especially my mom and
step father for the loan of their kitchen for the photo-shoot.
I'd especially like to thank 'Croapy' for her proof-reading skills.
Cheers JJ. Thanks also to Scott for checking the legalities of
what I'd written regarding the law and soap making.

Copyright © 2010 Joy James
All rights reserved. No part of this book may be reproduced
or transmitted in any form or by any means, electronic,
mechanical, photocopying, recording or otherwise, without
the prior written permission of How2crafts and Morse-Brown
Publishing.

Published by Morse-Brown Publishing
Series Editor: John Morse-Brown
Photography © Morse-Brown Design Limited
Design & Production: Morse-Brown Design Limited.
↗ www.morsebrowndesign.co.uk
For more titles in this series, see ↗ www.how2crafts.com

ISBN: 978-0-9550241-7-7

Notice of Liability. The information in this book is distributed
on an "as is" basis, without warranty. While every precaution
has been taken in the preparation of this book, the author Joy
James, How2crafts, Morse-Brown Publishing, their employees
or associates shall not have any liability to any person or entity
with respect to liability, loss, or damage caused or alleged to be
caused directly or indirectly by the instructions contained in this
book or by the products described herein.

Printed in Great Britain by the MPG Books Group,
Bodmin and King's Lynn

Durham County Council Libraries, Learning and Culture	
C0 1 69 68906 X5	
Askews	
668.1	

This is more than just a book...

This is the start of a conversation about making soap. By buying this book, you've joined that conversation, and we'd love to hear from you...

In this book you'll find photographic step-by-step instructions that will enable you to make amazing soap. But unlike most books you buy, it doesn't stop there. Once you've had a go at making soap yourself, you can upload and share photos of your soap, and any comments and ideas, onto our website at ↗ **www.how2crafts.com**. Then, once we've come to the end of the print run for this book, we'll select the best photos and comments and include them in the new edition of the book as a 'reader's appendix' – a source of inspiration and alternative designs for future readers.

As we've said on the how2crafts website, we believe crafts are all about conversation; the passing of skills and techniques from person to person down the ages. And we'd like our books to be part of that conversation. So it's only right that our books should change as the conversation progresses.

To join in the conversation visit
↗ **www.how2crafts.com**

Talk to us at
↗ **twitter.com/how2crafts**

Welcome to soap

This book is designed for the beginner soap maker. It shows the basic steps to making soap using the 'cold process' method. Using easily obtainable supplies you will be able to make a wonderful soap for your own personal use (any soap you make cannot legally be sold in the UK or EU without a Safety Assessment from a Certified Cosmetic Chemist and product liability insurance). Soap can easily be made in a kitchen using utensils that you are already likely to have or are easy to obtain (although if you intend to make soap on a regular basis then you will need to keep your soap making utensils separate from your cooking utensils).

We will be making three different types of cold process soap in this book, starting with a tried and tested recipe that works very well and uses easy-to-obtain ingredients. Each subsequent recipe will get a tad more adventurous, but all are well within the scope of a beginner. We will be using both an Essential Oil and Fragrance Oil (see glossary at the end of the book for a description of soaping terms).

The first recipe uses palm oil which is an excellent ingredient in soap-making as it saponifies easily (see glossary) but is, at this present moment in time, a bit controversial due to rainforests being cut down to make way for palm plantations for biofuels at the expense of orangutans and other native wildlife and endangered species. It is possible to buy palm oil (organic) from sustainable plantations where no virgin rainforest is being destroyed to grow palm and in some cases the farmers, especially those in Colombia, are being encouraged to grow sustainable palm rather than cocaine. This can be sourced from ↗ **www.fresholi.co.uk** but other soap making suppliers also supply organic palm oil from sustainable sources. Look for palm oil from suppliers that are signed up to the RSPO (Roundtable for Sustainable Palm Oil). One of the recipes doesn't contain palm oil for those of you who really don't want to use it.

Soap making has been around for a long time and it hasn't always been an easy thing to make, but with modern methods it is well within the scope of everybody.

What is soap?

In its very simplest terms, soap is made by mixing animal or vegetable oils or fats with lye (the common name for sodium hydroxide, also known as caustic soda) that has been dissolved in water. It is a chemical reaction which results in a completely new substance called soap, which is strictly speaking an alkali salt of a fatty acid.

Animal and vegetable fats are made up of fatty acids and glycerine. When the lye solution is mixed with the oils, the lye and fatty acids combine to make soap; some water and glycerine are left over from the process. This process is called saponification. The glycerine is retained in the soap making it nice and mild.

Soap is also a surfactant which enables water to more effectively wet things as water on its own doesn't wet things very well. There is a very complicated explanation as to how exactly soap works and it's all to do with molecules etc. but it is really beyond the scope of this book and in fact not really necessary to know but does make for fascinating reading.

Legend has it that soap was discovered in Rome under Mount Sapos, where the ashes from sacrificial fires would mix with the fats of sacrificed animals and wash downstream into a brook and that became the place of choice for Roman ladies to do their washing. This story is most likely fictitious, since there is documented use of soap as far back as 2500 B.C., way before the creation of the Roman Empire. Nonetheless, it does suggest how soap was probably first discovered – or rather, created.

For centuries, leftover, rendered fats from the farm and kitchen were the most likely ingredient for soap making. Soap making was a task most likely only performed once or twice a year. Lye was probably obtained by leaching water through wood ashes and collecting it in a pail under the ash box. Nowadays we can use a multitude of scrummy vegetable oils and butters to make our soap and never need to use animal fats, unless of course you want to. There are no animal fats used in any of the recipes in this book and neither do I use any animal fats in any of the soaps that I make.

Getting started

First of all you need to collect your equipment and ingredients together. I might add at this point that a notebook is a very handy item to have so you can jot down your findings and experiences whilst you are making your batches of soap. You can keep a note of your ingredients, additives, temperatures, the moulds you used etc. Trust me when I say "you'll never remember just how you made that fantastic soap a year down the line." Ask me how I know?

Personal safety when making soap is a primary concern. Lye (caustic soda) is extremely dangerous and I cannot stress enough the importance of wearing rubber gloves, goggles to protect the eyes, solid, sensible shoes on your feet, a face mask when mixing the caustic soda granules in water (it gives off some very nasty fumes for a few seconds), and old clothes and an apron. If you have long hair it would also be wise to tie it back or wear a hair-net. How cool is that?

I would recommend that all small children and pets are kept out of the room as well. It would only take a second for a nasty accident to happen.

Should you splash lye into your eyes or onto any other part of your body, wash the area thoroughly with copious amounts of water and seek medical advice straight away (especially in the case of your eyes).

If all these safety warnings and the fact that you now look like something from outer space haven't put you off we can get started on making soap.

But before you do, please read all the instructions first.

Equipment

- Safety equipment: rubber gloves, goggles, sensible shoes, face mask, old clothes, an apron and a hair net or hair band (optional).

- Plenty of old newspapers to cover your work surfaces.

- Disposable paper kitchen towels to mop up any spills and splashes.

- A bottle of white vinegar to neutralise any lye or raw soap splashes.

- A set of accurate, digital scales that have a 'tare' facility (return to zero), capable of measuring in 1 gram (1/12 oz) increments. These are fairly inexpensive and can be bought at large supermarket chains. I don't recommend the types that have a needle as they are just not accurate enough.

- A stainless steel saucepan large enough to hold all the oils and lye solution with space to stir without it slopping over the sides (3 – 4 litres). *Under no circumstances should you use an aluminium, cast iron or non-stick pan* as the lye will react with it and not only ruin the pan but the soap as well. If you want to use an enamel pan that is OK but make sure there are no chips in the enamel.

- An easy-to-read thermometer, preferably two. These can be simple kitchen or cook's thermometers used for jam making. You will need these to keep an eye on the temperature of both your lye and melted oils.

- Stainless steel or plastic spoons. Don't use wooden spoons as the lye reacts with the wood and you will eventually end up with wooden splinters in your soap.

- An all-in-one silicone spatula. Don't use the inexpensive rubber type, as they dissolve in lye. I found that out the hard way.

- Heat resistant plastic or ideally glass jugs.

- A mould to pour your soap into. I have very successfully used plastic boxes from ↗ **www.reallyusefulproducts.co.uk** (1.5L size is ideal) but any plastic container large

Equipment (continued)

enough to hold all the soap batter is fine as long as it is heat resistant. Wooden moulds can also be bought specially for soap but these need to be lined first with either cling film, a plastic bag, baking parchment or, as I prefer, freezer paper which can be bought from most quilt shops (see suppliers on page 42). I would also recommend lining the plastic boxes too. It makes removing the soap from the moulds easier. Please don't use metal moulds as new soap can react badly with metal. Silicone baking moulds are also fine to use but if you use these be aware that most of them are very flexible and would need to be put into a box or on a tray before you pour the soap batter into them, otherwise you'll have great difficulty in picking up the mould full of soap batter without spilling it.

I don't recommend using very small moulds whilst you are learning to make soap as these bring their own problems.

Make sure you have a small plastic container handy to pour excess batter into just in case your chosen mould won't hold all the batter.

A clean, empty margarine tub is ideal.

- A set of stainless steel measuring spoons. The sort that are nested together and measure 2.5ml (¼ teaspoon) upwards to 15ml (1 tablespoon).

- A sharp kitchen knife for slicing the unmoulded soap.

- A balloon whisk and/or a slotted spoon.

- A stick-blender or electric hand whisk (optional).

- Old towels to insulate the soap in the mould.

- Freezer paper/baking paper.

All the ingredients are to be weighed (including the water!) and please follow either the metric weight measurements or imperial weight measurements, not a mixture of both. Each recipe will use approximately 1 kg (2lb) of oils and this will produce approximately 12 100g (3½ oz) bars of soap.

Base oils

A quick word about the base oils we are going to use. Each oil requires a different amount of sodium hydroxide (lye) to turn it into soap. This is known as the SAP value of the oil. The recipes in this book are carefully calculated to turn only the oils stated in each of the recipes into soap and the oils are therefore not interchangeable. So don't substitute any of the oils as you may end up with either a very caustic soap or a very greasy soap that will go rancid and even develop orange spots (known affectionately as DOS – dreaded orange spots).

When calculating how much sodium hydroxide is needed to turn oils into soap we always allow a certain percentage of the oils to be left unsaponified, thereby making the soap moisturising. This percentage, anything from 5% to 8%, is known as the lye discount or the superfat amount. It can be very confusing when you start out but if you stick closely to these recipes until you are comfortable with the soap making process you won't go far wrong. Once you have become thoroughly addicted to soap making you will want to find out more and there

are numerous forums and websites dedicated to soap making for you to study on the web.

Olive oil (see ① overleaf) contributes a rich, creamy lather without too many bubbles, and is known for its highly moisturising and mild cleansing properties. I like to use the light, grade A olive oil – not extra virgin oil but the next one down. It is possible to use all grades of olive oil from extra virgin to pomace, but I have had the best results from the light olive oil. Pomace olive oil is extracted using solvents and whilst it makes great soap it can react with some Fragrance and Essential Oils, turning soap into what is known as 'soap in a pot', where the soap batter solidifies almost instantaneously. If you want bigger bubbles, try combining olive oil with other oils like coconut oil and palm oil for example. One final point: When buying olive oil make sure it is pure olive oil and not a blend of olive oil with something else.

Coconut oil (see ② overleaf) comes from crushed copra, the dried, white meat of the kernels of the coconut palm. It produces a rich

Base oils (continued)

lather with lots of big bubbles. It adds hardness to a bar of soap and is highly moisturising. It is said to be the only oil that if made into soap will lather in salt water.

Palm oil ③ is produced from the pulp and flesh of the oil palm. It is high in fatty acids and vitamin E. It is a popular choice for the soap maker as it saponifies easily and makes a nice hard bar of soap. It is known as the vegetable alternative to tallow. Make sure you buy the refined oil as the unrefined oil is very orange and will give your soap an orange cast (unless of course that is what you want) or it could be mixed with refined palm to produce a pale yellow soap. See note about growing...

Cocoa butter ④ is pressed from the cocoa bean. It has a rich, chocolatey aroma. It is prized for its skin-softening and healing properties. It is a hard, white, brittle fat that helps to make a moisturising, hard bar of soap. Deodorised cocoa butter is also available.

Castor oil ⑤ is a thick, clear, viscous liquid that is pressed from the castor bean. It is a very moisturising, lubricating oil. It acts as a humectant, attracting moisture to your skin. It produces a wonderfully emollient, hard bar of soap with lots and lots of fluffy, creamy lather.

Shea butter ⑥ is pressed from the pits of the fruit of the African butter tree. It is also known as African Karite Butter. It is a gorgeous, creamy butter that melts on skin contact. It is very moisturising and gentle and is excellent for people with dry skin conditions. It adds a real touch of luxury to soap.

Rice bran oil ⑦ is high in fatty acids with anti-oxidising properties and some sunscreen properties. It is very good for sensitive, mature, or delicate skin or where additional moisturising is desired. It is a nice, emollient oil to use in soap making.

Wheatgerm oil ⑧ is very rich in vitamin E. It can be used to nourish dry or cracked skin and is known to soothe skin problems such as eczema and psoriasis. It is reputed to help prevent and reduce scarring and may even prevent stretch marks. Mature skin, in particular, will benefit from wheatgerm oil.

Additives

In each of these three recipes there is the opportunity to add either oatmeal, wheatgerm flakes, honey, crushed rosehips or lavender buds. These are entirely optional and won't adversely affect the quality of your soap if you leave them out. But they will either add texture or extra properties to your soap bars should you want to include them.

Lavender buds Ⓐ can be ground in a coffee bean grinder and a small amount added to the soap batter for texture and gentle exfoliation or they can be left whole and sprinkled on top of the soap once it has been poured into the mould. If you include whole buds in the soap batter they will turn brown and resemble mouse poo.

Honey Ⓑ can impart a light, warm, sweet scent and acts as a humectant. I generally use about 1 tablespoon per kilo (2lbs) of oils and add it at a very, very light trace. You want to make sure it gets completely incorporated into the soap before your trace gets too thick otherwise it won't incorporate properly and you may end up with honey streaks in your soap. Honey will turn your soap a light tan colour.

Don't be tempted to add more honey to your soap batter to get a stronger honey fragrance as honey has a very nasty habit of overheating and turning, at best, your soap into a volcano or at worst a gooey mess that is totally unusable. I usually add a small amount of honey Fragrance Oil to my soap to give me the desired fragrance. There are some very realistic Fragrance Oils about and my favourite comes from
↗ **www.gracefruit.com**

Oatmeal Ⓒ is excellent for dry, itchy skin. It acts as a very gentle exfoliator and very good for sensitive skin.

Wheatgerm Flakes Ⓓ give a nice texture and gentle exfoliating quality to the soap. They are also full of vitamin E which is very good for the skin. The flakes also impart a nice speckled, golden colour to your soap.

Rosehips Ⓔ Rosehip oil is rich in vitamin C, and when the rosehips are crushed and added to soap, they impart a nice warm browny-pink colour, as well as a scrubby feel to your soap.

Fragrancing

There are two main ways to add fragrance to your soap – Essential Oils and Fragrance Oils. I shall cover both types briefly here. In the UK and EU there is a legal limit on how much either Fragrance or Essential Oil you can use in soap. For all Fragrance Oils it is 3% of your total recipe amount, including the water. If you use the full 3% of your Fragrance Oil it will be a very strong smelling soap and I have never used that amount yet. So what I do is use 3% of the total oil weight; for example, 30 grams to one kilo of oils. This is more than enough to get a nice fragrance without removing the hairs from your nose. Essential Oils are different, see below.

Essential Oils are potent natural substances, and used incorrectly they can cause adverse reactions. Some, such as the citrus oils, can cause phototoxicity; some are not good for people with high blood pressure, if you are pregnant, nursing, suffer with epilepsy, etc. The law in the UK and EU is very strict about the levels of Essential Oils that can be used in cosmetics. I suggest that if the Essential Oil route is the way you wish to go to fragrance your soaps then you will need to do a good deal of research first.

I have used lavender Essential Oil in one of the recipes in this book as it is a pretty safe oil to use and very popular, with excellent calming, cleansing and sleep-inducing properties. At this point I would like to add that it is not known how much of the properties of the Essential Oils are still active in soap after it has been through the saponification process.

I have listed a couple of Essential Oils that are fine to use at the maximum of 3% if you wish to try them. And when I say 3%, that is the maximum you can use either combined or singularly.

Lavender Essential Oil Ⓕ (Lavandula augustifolia) is a calming, relaxing oil, which combats stress, while its antiseptic properties help with colds, flu and other ailments. It is excellent for asthma and migraine sufferers. It also aids sleep.

Geranium Essential Oil Ⓖ (Pelargonium graveolens) is good for problem skins such as acne, congestion and oiliness as well as being a good choice for mature skin. It is also good for skin conditions such as dermatitis and eczema, broken capillaries and is soothing to dry, sensitive skin. It is also said to stimulate the regeneration of skin cells.

Note: Both lavender and geranium blend well together – try mixing them at 50/50.

Fragrance Oils – Fragrance Oils are a blend of both natural and synthetic ingredients. They are very stable and there is no variation from one batch of Fragrance Oil to another, unlike Essential Oils which will vary due to their nature. They are formulated to be skin-safe and are designed to be used in a variety of ways, from scenting soaps, shampoos and bath bombs to candles. They can be used at the rate of 3% in soaps and other wash-off body products. They come in a vast array of scents – from crisp apples to strawberries and champagne and everything in between. There are many very reputable sellers of Fragrance Oils suitable for use in soap and if you wish to use them then please make sure you are buying skin-safe, IFRA (International Fragrance Association) approved oils and not potpourri oils. Most Fragrance Oil suppliers rigorously test their oils in CP soap before selling them so they know how they react in the soap mixture.

Rose Fragrance Oil Ⓗ

Colouring

There are many safe ways to colour your soap, please do not be tempted to grate wax crayons to colour your soaps. Wax crayons are not skin-safe.

It is possible to use herbs, spices and roots infused in oils, dried vegetable powders such as carrot and tomato, cocoa and carob powder, synthetic, skin-safe colours designed to stay true in the alkaline environment of raw soap, clays, ultramarines, oxides and lakes.

If you are looking for soft, gentle, natural colours then herbs, spices, roots, dried vegetable powders, cocoa and carob powders are probably the best. Ultramarines are also soft and gentle. Clays also give nice soft colours and also impart extra qualities to your soap.

If you are looking for more vibrant colours then you will need to use the synthetic colourants. Oxides and lakes also give fairly strong colours and are, in my opinion, much more difficult to use, especially for the beginner.

The Recipes
1. White Lavender Soap

Ingredients	Metric	Imperial
Olive oil	400 grams	14 oz
Coconut oil	300 grams	10½ oz
Palm oil	250 grams	9 oz
Cocoa butter	50 grams	2 oz
Caustic soda	142 grams	5 oz
Water	367 grams	13 oz
Lavender Essential Oil	30 grams	1½ oz
Oatmeal (optional)	5 grams	¼ oz
Lavender buds (optional)	(either whole buds to sprinkle on the top, or ground to mix in to the soap batter).	

Method. Follow the basic method from page 22. When you have achieved trace (see the explanation for this on page 28) add the lavender Essential Oil, oatmeal (optional) and ground lavender buds (optional). If you are adding ground lavender buds, err on the side of caution – less is better.

When the Essential Oil and optional additives have been fully stirred in, begin to pour your soap into the mould (see page 30).

NB. *If you have added oatmeal to your soap you may find that when the new soap is de-moulded and cut into bars it will have an odd smell. This will last for a few days or more but it will eventually disappear.*

Options. Instead of using only lavender Essential Oil, try mixing it 50/50 with geranium Essential Oil, or using an oatmeal, milk and honey Fragrance Oil instead.

2. Honey and Wheatgerm Soap

Ingredients	Metric	Imperial
Olive oil	400 grams	14 oz
Coconut oil	300 grams	10½ oz
Palm oil	200 grams	7 oz
Cocoa butter	50 grams	2 oz
Wheatgerm oil	30 grams	1½ oz
Castor oil	20 grams	1 oz
Caustic soda	141 grams	5 oz
Water	366 grams	13½ oz
Wheatgerm flakes	15 grams	½ oz or 1 tablespoon
Runny honey	10 grams/ml	2 teaspoons

Method. Follow the basic method from page 22 up to the end of page 26. When you have achieved a light trace (page 28) add the honey. It may help to warm the honey up slightly so that it incorporates better into the soap batter. Add the wheatgerm powder and mix in thoroughly, making sure there are no lumps. The batter will turn a beautiful golden colour. When the honey and wheatgerm flakes have been fully incorporated, then begin to pour your soap into the mould (page 30).

NB. *If you have added wheatgerm flakes to your soap you may find that when the new soap is de-moulded and cut into bars it will have an odd smell. This will last for a few days or more but it will eventually disappear.*

Options. Try adding some orange or lemon Fragrance Oil to this soap – 30 ml or 1½ oz. Please note I have said Fragrance Oil NOT Essential Oil, as citrus Essential Oil is one of those Essential Oils that is restricted by law.

3. Palm-free Rose Soap

Ingredients	Metric	Imperial
Olive oil	435 grams	16 oz
Coconut oil	348 grams	13 oz
Rice bran oil	130 grams	5 oz
Shea butter	87 grams	3 oz
Water	382 grams	14 oz
Caustic soda	139 grams	5 oz
Rose Fragrance Oil	30 grams	1½ oz
Fine cut rosehips (optional)	5 grams	1 teaspoon

Method. Follow the basic method from page 22 up to the end of page 26, except let your oils and lye cool to a lower temperature of somewhere between 25°C (80°F) and 30°C (90°F). When the soap has reached a thin trace (see page 28), add the rosehips if required, and the Fragrance Oil, stirring well with a slotted spoon, not a stick-blender.

The reason for the lower temperature is that floral Fragrance Oils can accelerate trace and before you know it, you have a solid mass of soap in your pan – known in the trade as 'soap in a pot'.

When the rosehips and Fragrance Oil have been fully incorporated then continue to pour your soap into the mould (page 30).

Options. You can substitute any Fragrance Oil for the rose Fragrance Oil. You may even wish to have a go at colouring this soap. Please be aware that some Fragrance Oils will colour your soap as well as fragrance them, especially those that contain any hint of vanilla. Check with your Fragrance Oil supplier to see if the oils you have purchased are ones that will change your soap's colour. It would be a useless exercise to colour a soap pale pink when the Fragrance Oil changes it to dark brown.

The basic method

This is the basic method for all three recipes. The photos refer to the white lavender soap recipe on page 16, but all three soaps can be made from the instructions. Options that are particular to each soap are listed on the individual recipe pages (pages 16, 18 and 20).

Remove all cats, dogs and children from the work area. Clear your workspace, wipe the surfaces down with an antibacterial spray (some people may think this is unnecessary but I like to ensure I start clean).

Line your chosen mould or moulds, if required, with either freezer paper, baking parchment or your chosen method (Figs 1 & 2).

Now cover your work area with a couple of layers of old newspaper.

Collect everything you are going to need in one area. There is nothing more frustrating than finding you have forgotten something (a Fragrance Oil for example) just as you are ready to pour your soap. Or in my case after you've poured it. Trust me – I have made beautifully coloured and swirled soap with no fragrance, just because I had forgotten my Fragrance Oil.

Now put on the safety gear.

Weigh out the caustic soda (Fig 3). It is very important to keep the caustic soda covered at all times, as it attracts moisture and this would give rise to inaccuracies when weighing it.

Next weigh out the water into a separate jug (Fig 4). You can use tap water if you live in a soft water area but if you live in a hard water area you might want to think about using bottled water or even distilled water.

Add the caustic soda to the water (Fig 5), (not the other way round), and stir continuously to prevent the soda from solidifying into a thick, ice-like mass at the bottom of the jug. You may need to turn your head away so that you don't breathe in the fumes.

You have now created a lye solution: caustic soda in water in other words.

The chemical reaction of the soda hitting the water will heat the lye solution up to near boiling point.

Put the lye solution on a window sill (Fig 6), or somewhere where it's in no danger of being knocked over, to cool down.

Weigh out the solid oils first (Figs 7 & 8) and place them over a gentle heat to melt them. Once melted, remove the oils from the heat.

Weigh out the liquid oils next and add these to the melted hard oils (Fig 9). You can, if you wish, put both the solid and liquid oils in the pan together and heat them both at the same time. I just prefer to do it the other way, as adding the liquid oils to the melted solid oils brings the temperature of the melted oils down nicely, which is what needs to happen next...

This next step is a bit of a juggling act. You need the temperature of the lye and the temperature of the melted oils to be approximately the same, at 40°C (104°F). This temperature is ideal for most soaps. (It works well for me, but you may find that other soap making sources will vary in their temperature recommendations.) In order to get both the lye and the melted oils to the same temperature (Fig 10) you can either heat or cool the lye as necessary, using a hot or cold water bath. A washing-up bowl or sink will do for this.

Once you have got your oils and lye to approximately the same temperature (within a degree or two) then you can pour the lye into the melted oils (Fig 11).

Stir continuously (Fig 12) until the mixture 'traces'. 'Trace' is achieved when the mixture thickens and reaches a consistency whereby if you drizzle some of the batter off a spoon on to the batter surface, the drizzled batter is momentarily visible on the surface (Fig 14). You are basically looking for a thin to medium custard consistency. Trace can take minutes, or if you are using a recipe with a high percentage of olive oil in, it may take hours. Just keep stirring! You may prefer to use a stick-blender or electric whisk (Fig 13), although they need to be used with caution as you can go from no trace to a very thick trace, very quickly. Take care also that you don't whisk too vigorously and end up with soap batter all over the kitchen. A deep pan or pot is therefore better than a shallow one for this.

If using a stick-blender, I recommend that you blend for 5 seconds and stir for 5 seconds (using the blender as a stirring tool), and repeat until trace is achieved.

Fig 14 shows the moment when trace is achieved. If you look closely you can see lines on the surface of the soap batter.

Next you need to add any Essential Oils or
Fragrance Oils, colourings or other additives to
the soap batter (Fig 15). For the exact quantities
see the individual recipes on pages 14–18.
Then stir these additives in well with your
spatula (Fig 16).

Once anything else has been added then you
can pour your soap into your chosen mould
(Fig 17). Get that spatula and scrape every last bit
of soap batter into the mould.

If the recipe calls for lavender buds then this is the time to sprinkle them on the surface of the soap (Fig 18). You want a density similar to that shown in Fig 19.

Now cover the top of the mould with a piece of cardboard (Fig 20). If you're using a plastic container I don't recommend that you put the lid on as the soap may overheat or you may get condensation that will drip onto the top of the soap. It doesn't affect the quality of the soap but it doesn't look very nice.

Put the soap in the mould somewhere out of drafts and harm's way and cover with an old towel or two to insulate it (Fig 21).

Now is the cleaning up bit. Wearing your rubber gloves clean any excess soap batter out of your pan or off your utensils with paper kitchen towels and dispose of in the bin. Don't pour any excess soap batter down the sink as it will block it. Next wash all your utensils in a bowl or sink of hot, soapy water. Dispose of all your newspapers you used to cover your work surfaces.

Now the hard part – leave it alone for at least 24 hours. Should you peek at your soap in the mould during this time (and I know you will because I still do!), you may notice that it has become very hot, especially if you have used a spicy or floral scent. It will have also become almost translucent. This is the soap going through what is known as 'gel'. Don't worry – this is what it is supposed to do and is completely normal. (There may be instances as you get more expert at making soap and you want to experiment with other ingredients where you don't want to let the soap 'gel' and this is OK too.) In Fig 22 you can see the gel hasn't yet reached the very outer edges.

After at least 24 hours your soap will be ready to un-mould. It should have the consistency of a firm cheddar cheese (Fig 23). If you have made a palm-free soap you may find that it is a bit stickier. It will soon harden up.

You may now cut your soap into bars or whatever shape you want (Fig 24). When handling new soap don't forget to wear your rubber gloves as the soap will still be a bit harsh on the skin. Leave your newly cut works of art somewhere nice, airy and cool to dry out for 4 – 6 weeks before using.

If you really can't wait that long to see if your soap really does lather and bubble then by all means don your rubber gloves and lather away. If you get nice creamy bubbles then feel free to do a 'Happy Dance' around the kitchen and have a cuppa to celebrate.

Finally, why not upload a photo of your soap on to the how2crafts website? You'll be in with a chance of getting in to the next edition of this book... ↗ **www. how2crafts.com/contribute**

Glossary

Cold Process (CP) A method of soap making without using any external heat source.

DOS Dreaded Orange Spots. Small dark orange spots that usually occur on the surface of cold processed soap. The primary cause is most likely to be unsaponified oils turning rancid.

Emollient An additive used to soften or soothe your skin. Cocoa or Shea butters are often added to handmade soaps as an emollient.

Essential Oil (EO) Highly concentrated, volatile oil extracted from aromatic plants, most commonly through pressing or steam distillation. They are used for fragrancing and more commonly aromatherapy treatments. Some are also used as flavourings.

Exfoliant An abrasive added to soap to slough off dead skin cells, such as oatmeal, wheatgerm or poppy seeds, etc.

Fragrance Oil (FO) Synthetic oils formulated to mimic natural fragrances. They are quite often blended with Essential Oils.

Gel Gel is what happens after the soap has been poured into the mould. It will get so hot that it almost liquefies and turns translucent. It really does look like a gel. It usually starts with a dark appearance in the middle of the mould and it works its way outwards to the edges. Once cool it will harden and turn opaque.

Hot process soap This is a type of CP soap that is then cooked in a slow-cooker. It is able to be used almost straight away but tends to give more 'rustic' looking bars.

Humectant A substance that attracts and holds moisture unto itself, such as glycerine or honey.

INCI Name International Nomenclature of Cosmetic Ingredients. The INCI name (see ↗ **bit.ly/INCIng**) is required by law when labelling cosmetics marketed in the UK and EU. This may also be needed in other countries.

Lye The common name for sodium hydroxide, also known as caustic soda.

Olive pomace oil Pomace is the ground flesh and pits after pressing. Olive-pomace oil is the oil obtained by treating olive pomace with solvents or other physical treatments. It is considered an inferior grade and is used for soap making or industrial purposes.

SAP Value Saponification value. The amount of potassium hydroxide in milligrams required to saponify 1 gram of oil.

Saponification The process or reaction of combining a base (fat) with an alkali (sodium hydroxide) to produce a salt (soap) and a free alcohol (glycerine).

Seize The unexpected thickening and hardening of the soap mixture in the pot during stirring. It looks very similar to curdled milk. It is usually caused when adding certain synthetic Fragrance Oils or spicy Essential Oils to the mixture.

Superfat The addition of extra oils or butters which remain unsaponified within the finished soap. These excess oils and butters contribute to the moisturising properties of the soap.

Surfactant A substance that reduces the surface tension of a liquid in which it is dissolved, such as a detergent or soap.

Trace The point in soap making where the mixture reaches a certain consistency or thickness that is most noticeable when the soap is drizzled upon itself and leaves a trail before disappearing back into the mixture.

Unsaponifiables Components that do not react with caustic soda (sodium hydroxide) during saponification and remain in their original state. These components contribute moisturising or other skin nourishing properties to the finished soap.

Troubleshooting

As with all handmade products, things do sometimes go wrong with soap making. I've put together the following troubleshooting guide for any botched batches you might end up with.

1. Always check your recipe.

To borrow a term I use when teaching patchwork, *measure twice, cut once*. Measure all your ingredients accurately, and then do it again, to make sure you have accurately measured the right ingredient.

2. How accurate are your scales?

If you are in any doubt as to the accuracy of your scales get them tested. I also prefer to use grams (metric) rather than ounces (imperial) as it's easier to be accurate with grams in my opinion.

3. Did you forget something?

It is very easy to forget to add an ingredient in soap making, especially if you get distracted – by the phone for example.

4. Heat issues. Many problems are caused by too much heat being lost during stirring,

or because of inadequate insulation when the soap is in the mould. (As with just about everything there are exceptions to this rule, especially for those soap makers who make milk soaps and freeze the milk and don't allow the soap to gel. This is a fairly advanced technique for experienced soap makers and is not covered here.) The most common heat problem is heat loss during stirring. This is most likely to happen if you are hand-stirring your soap (rather than using a stick-blender), working with small batches, or making a soap that is high in an oil that is very slow to trace such as olive oil. To avoid heat-loss during stirring, use a stick-blender to speed the stirring up.

The second most common problem is heat loss when the soap is in the mould. When soap is made properly it will heat up in the mould – this is a part of the saponification process. It is important to retain this heat by covering the mould with towels to insulate it. As the soap in the mould heats up, it will go through what is known as gel (see the description on page 34 and the glossary on page 36).

The first time you witness a gel phase it can be alarming, and you may think something is wrong with your soap. It will start to get darker in the centre and become translucent, the darker bit being melted raw soap. This gelling will spread from the centre to cover the whole surface, and throughout the soap. Once the soap has completely cooled down the opaque appearance will return and the colour will lighten considerably. Soap that has gone through gel will be a darker colour when finished than soap that has never gelled. Some colorants rely on the soap going through the gel phase to achieve the correct colour. This is especially true of synthetic colorants.

If after doing all of this you still have botched batches, then the following is a list of symptoms and possible causes.

Problems in the soap pot

1. My soap won't trace.

If your soap won't trace it may be because there is either insufficient lye, too much water, it's at the wrong temperature, it's not been stirred enough or it's been stirred too slowly. A high percentage of olive oil will also cause slow tracing if you are stirring your soap by hand rather than with a stick-blender. Double-check the quantities of water, oil and lye. If the amounts and temperatures are correct, continue stirring intermittently until the solution traces. If possible, use a stick-blender, which will substantially speed up trace.

2. My soap batter looks like cottage cheese.

This means your soap batter has seized. This is probably due to the addition of a fragrance or Essential Oil (florals and spicy ones are notorious for this). It can also happen if the temperatures of the lye solution and the oils were wildly different when you mixed them. You may be able to rescue the soap if you use a stick-blender. Blend it until it is smooth and get it into the mould as quickly as possible.

3. The oils and lye have separated.
If this happens, the lye solution and oils have not been stirred enough – keep stirring until you achieve trace.

4. My batter looks curdled.
This could mean the batter is on its way to seizing. Try mixing with a firm hand and then pour.

5. My additives have sunk to the bottom.
If additives (e.g. oatmeal, etc) have sunk, it's probably because you added them when your soap batter was too thin. Keep stirring until a heavier trace is achieved and they will eventually move throughout the batter and remain suspended.

Problems in the mould

1. Lye water is floating on the top of an oily mass. This is most likely caused by you not stirring enough and achieving trace. Pour the batter back into the pan and stir again until trace is achieved.

2. A thick layer of oil is floating on the top of a saponified mass. This is probably due to insufficient stirring before you poured the soap, and/or a false trace. It may also be due to inaccurate measurements. This soap is likely to be too harsh and is best thrown away.

Problems after removing from the mould

1. There is a layer of white powder on the top of my soap.
This is known as 'ash'. It doesn't mean the soap is bad or harmful, and you can just wash it off. I sometimes get it on one batch and not on the next, even when making two batches of identical soap on the same day.

2. When I cut the soap there are small pockets filled with liquid. These are known as 'lye pockets' and are most likely caused by insufficient stirring of the soap batter before pouring it into the mould. The bars of soap are likely to be unsafe and it would be best to discard them.

This is by no means a comprehensive list of problems that can arise when making soap. I can only suggest you read lots, join soap making forums and generally find out as much as you can. There are many very lively forums and discussion groups on the web where you can ask for or offer advice. I have listed a few on page 43.

Suppliers

United Kingdom
Very high quality raw ingredients, allergen free Fragrance Oils and Essential Oils:
- ↗ **www.fresholi.co.uk**

Raw ingredients, fragrances and Essential Oils:
- ↗ **www.justasoap.co.uk**
- ↗ **www.gracefruit.com**
- ↗ **www.thesoapkitchen.co.uk**
- ↗ **www.soapmakers-store.com**

Custom made wooden moulds:
- ↗ **www.lomondsoap.com**

Fragrance Oil specialist and candle making supplies:
- ↗ **www.sensoryperfection.co.uk**

Freezer paper supplier
- ↗ **www.riodesigns.co.uk**

Cosmetic Safety Assessments
- ↗ **www.soapschool.com**
- ↗ **www.cosmeticsafetyassessment.com**

USA
Comprehensive line of soap making supplies and soap making products, including Fragrance Oil, Essential Oil, soap pigments, colorants etc.
- ↗ **www.brambleberry.com**

Canada
Supplier of raw ingredients, fragrance and Essential Oils.
- ↗ **www.sudsandscents.com**

Australia
Aussie Soap Supplies is your "One Stop Online Shop" for Soap and Lotion making supplies.
- ↗ **www.aussiesoapsupplies.com.au**

EU
Austria: ↗ **www.kosmetikmacherei.at /html**
Germany: ↗ **www.macsoapy.de**
Finland: ↗ **www.tuoksukauppa.net**
Switzerland: ↗ **www.allerlei-praktisches.ch**
France: ↗ **www.macosmetoperso.com**
Spain: ↗ **www.atumaneramanualidades.com**
Estonia: ↗ **www.hobipunkt.ee**

Forums and useful links

Soap making forums
Very friendly forum open to everybody:
↗ **www.forum.fresholi.co.uk**

Other friendly, knowledgeable forums:
↗ **www.soapmakingforum.com**
↗ **www.thedishforum.com**

Useful Links
Useful site for USA readers regarding the labelling of soap and other cosmetics:
↗ **bit.ly/cosmeticlabels**

About the author

Joy James is a self-confessed craft-a-holic, having crafted nearly all her life. She has taught several different crafts, both privately and for a further education college where she was also an internal verifier for the City and Guilds Creative courses. She taught Patchwork and Quilting at OCN level 2 for the college and it pleases her greatly that the ladies still meet several years later. She still teaches private groups now and again.

Joy first discovered soap making whilst working as a Marketing and Events Assistant for the Made in Lancashire Art & Craft Initiative. One of the members (thanks Sue!) made soap and it intrigued Joy no end. Sue gave her a bar of patchouli soap and Joy was in love. When Joy had to leave that job and move to Derbyshire with her husband due to a change in his job, she decided to have a go at making soap whilst looking for a new job. She was hooked from the word go and hasn't stopped making it since. She now has a very clean family and set of friends...